Alfred's

Music for Little Mozarts

A Halloween Story with Performance Music
and Related Music Activity Pages

Alfred

Christine H. Barden · Gayle Kowalchyk · E. L. Lancaster

Beethoven Bear and Mozart Mouse and the Perfect Pumpkin

It was a beautiful, sunny autumn day. Beethoven Bear and Mozart Mouse were looking out the playroom window. The trees in the backyard were bright with the colors of fall—all different shades of red, orange and gold. The children were there, raking the fallen leaves into big piles. Every now and then, they would run and jump into the pile, only to scatter the leaves in all directions. Then they would rake some more.

"That looks like so much fun," Beethoven Bear sighed. "I wish we could go outside and play."

"Me, too," Mozart Mouse agreed. Then he added, "I love this time of year." He paused for a moment. "Hey!" he exclaimed. "I just thought of something. If it's time to rake leaves, then that means only one thing."

"What?" asked Beethoven Bear, sounding puzzled.

"It's almost time for Halloween!" Mozart Mouse announced.

"Halloween!" Beethoven Bear repeated. "That means dressing up in costumes and trick-or-treating for lots of candy. Mmm." His tummy began to rumble with the thought of all those goodies.

"And don't forget the pumpkins," Mozart Mouse reminded him. "It's not Halloween if we don't have pumpkins to carve into Jack-o-Lanterns."

Beethoven Bear's smile faded. "Pumpkins? How are we going to get pumpkins?" he asked his friend.

Just then, the children ran into the playroom and scooped up the little bear and mouse. "We're going to the pumpkin patch!" they said excitedly. "And you are going with us!"

"Hooray!" shouted Beethoven Bear and Mozart Mouse as they eagerly began another adventure together.

> **To the Teacher:** Use *Music for Little Mozarts Halloween Fun! Book 1* during the Halloween season while the student is studying pages 19–25 in the Music Lesson Book 1, or as a review any time after page 25. Students will enjoy the Halloween story with its related pictures and activity pages. Many will also want to color the illustrations found throughout the story. Happy Halloween!

After a beautiful drive on country roads through colorful farmland, they finally arrived at the pumpkin patch. Beethoven Bear and Mozart Mouse looked around in amazement. Beethoven Bear gave a low whistle. "I've never seen so many pumpkins in one place!" he exclaimed.

Mozart Mouse couldn't believe his eyes. "There are pumpkins everywhere," he replied.

1. Place Beethoven Bear on 2 black keys.
2. Clap (or tap) *Pumpkins Everywhere* and count aloud evenly.
3. Point to the quarter notes & rests below and count aloud evenly.
4. Say the finger numbers aloud while playing them in the air.
5. Play using RH & LH and say the finger numbers.
6. Play and sing the words.

Pumpkins Everywhere

Student plays two octaves higher with duet part.

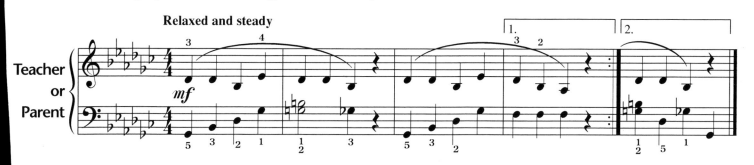

"**W**ith all of these pumpkins, it should be easy to find just the right one," said Mozart Mouse.

"Which way should we go?" asked Beethoven Bear. "It looks like there are different paths."

"Let's start over here," Mozart Mouse suggested. "Hurry, my friend. Let's find the perfect pumpkin!"

The Path to the Perfect Pumpkin

Help Mozart Mouse and Beethoven Bear find the perfect pumpkin by following the path that has signs containing this rhythm:

❶ Draw a line along the path.

❷ Stop along the way to clap and count each pattern aloud.

❸ Then color the picture.

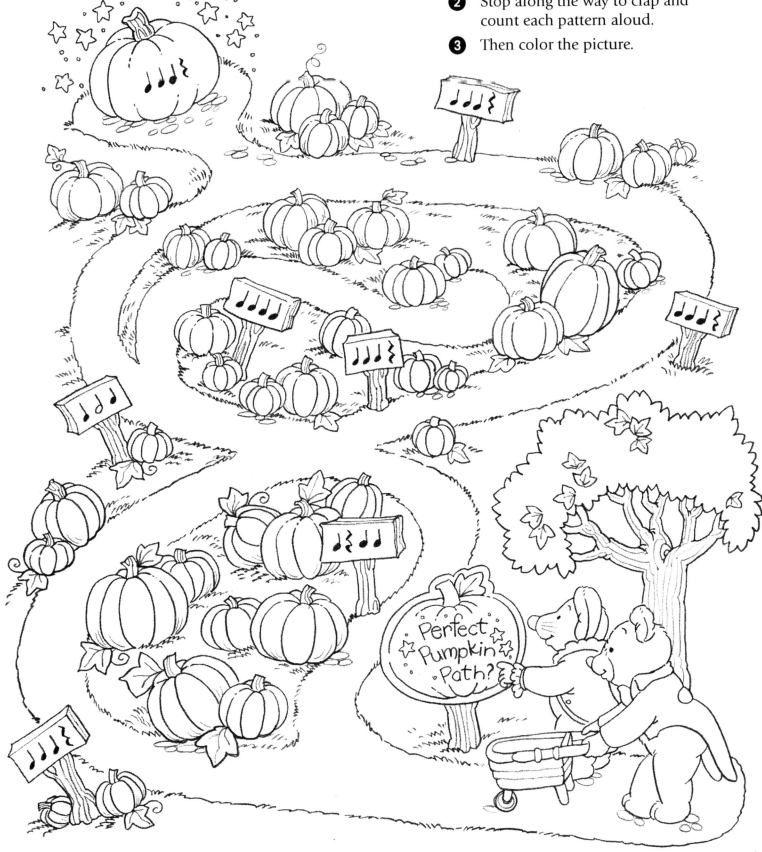

Finding the perfect pumpkin wasn't as easy as it first seemed. Some were too big, some were too little, and some had funny shapes. But just as they were about to give up, Beethoven Bear shouted, "Look at that one!" They both ran to see it.

"You did it!" exclaimed Mozart Mouse. "You found the only perfect pumpkin in the patch!"

They put the pumpkin between them for the ride back home. After so much excitement, it wasn't long before they both fell fast asleep. Mozart Mouse dreamed of all the funny faces he could carve on their perfect pumpkin, to make a Jack-o-Lantern. Beethoven Bear, whose thoughts were never far from food, dreamed about the yummy pumpkin pie they could make. And of course, it would be topped with lots of fluffy, whipped cream.

The Perfect Pumpkin Pie

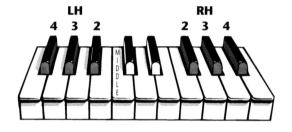

1. Place Mozart Mouse on 3 black keys.
2. Clap (or tap) *The Perfect Pumpkin Pie* and count aloud evenly.
3. Point to the quarter notes & rests below and count aloud evenly.
4. Say the finger numbers aloud while playing them in the air.
5. Play using RH & LH and say the finger numbers.
6. Play and sing the words.

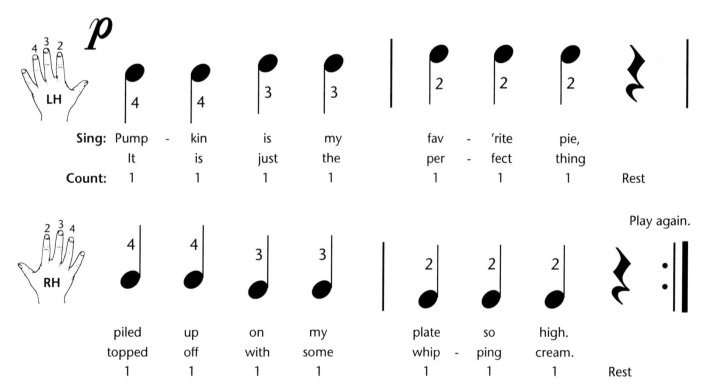

Student plays two octaves higher with duet part.

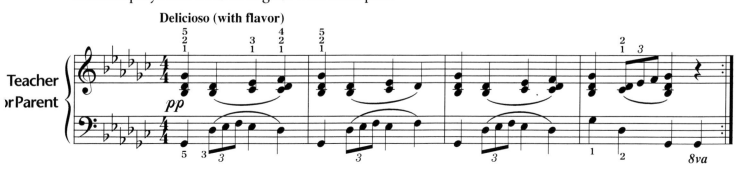

As soon as they got home, Beethoven Bear and Mozart Mouse got ready to carve their pumpkin. They spread newspaper on the floor. Together, they drew a face on the pumpkin. Then they carefully carved two eyes, a nose and a toothy grin. They stepped back to admire their work.

"This is the best Jack-o-Lantern ever!" declared Beethoven Bear.

1. Color the areas containing a QUARTER NOTE (♩) **green**.
2. Color the areas containing a QUARTER REST (𝄽) **gray**.
3. Color the areas containing a 2-BLACK-KEY GROUP **black**.
4. Color the areas containing a 3-BLACK-KEY GROUP **orange**.
5. Color the areas containing a FORTE SIGN (*f*) **brown**.
6. Color the areas containing a PIANO SIGN (*p*) **yellow**.
7. Then color the rest of the picture.

The Best Jack-o-Lantern

Later, they gathered all their toy friends from the playroom and made a pumpkin pie. Everyone helped. Finally, it was ready to eat. Mozart Mouse cut a piece for everyone, and Beethoven Bear put a generous topping of whipped cream on each slice.

"Yum!" said Beethoven Bear. "I could eat this all day."

Mozart Mouse giggled as some whipped cream made its way to the tip of Beethoven Bear's nose. "Is this your favorite part of Halloween?" he asked his friend.

"I can think of something even better than this," he answered. He looked around the room and smiled. "My favorite part of Halloween isn't carving the pumpkin, eating pumpkin pie or even trick-or-treating. My favorite part of Halloween is being with friends like you."

1. Place Beethoven Bear on 2 black keys and Mozart Mouse on 3 black keys.
2. Clap (or tap) *Friends Like You* and count aloud evenly.
3. Point to the quarter notes & rest below and count aloud evenly.
4. Say the finger numbers aloud while playing them in the air.
5. Play using RH & LH and say the finger numbers.
6. Play and sing the words.

Friends Like You

Sing:	Jack	-	o	-	lan	-	terns,		trick	-	or	-	treat	-	ing,
	pump	-	kin		pie		that's		good		for		eat	-	ing,
	sil	-	ly		cos	-	tumes,		can	-	dy,		too,		but
Count:	1		1		1		1		1		1		1		1

| | best | of | all | are | friends | like | you. | |
| | 1 | 1 | 1 | 1 | 1 | 1 | 1 | Rest |

Student plays one octave higher with duet part.

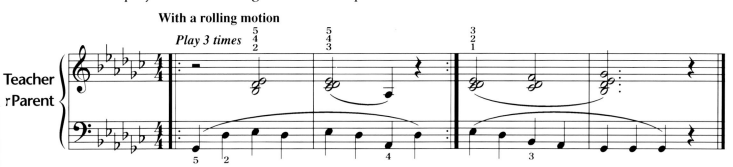

Compact Discs/ General MIDI Disks

All the music from the Music Lesson & Music Discovery Books, plus more

CDs
Book 1 (14578)
Book 2 (14582)
Book 3 (17184)
Book 4 (17190)

GM Disks
Book 1 (14658)
Book 2 (14659)
Book 3 (17185)
Book 4 (17191)

Flash Cards
Music terms and symbols, rhythm patterns

Book 1 (14587)   Book 3 (17183)
Book 2 (14599)   Book 4 (17189)

Starter Kit
Tote Bag, Beethoven Bear and Mozart Mouse Plush Toys, Music Activity Board (14586)

Deluxe Starter Kit
Same as above, plus Book 1 of the Music Lesson Book, Music Workbook, Music Discovery Book, Flash Cards and Compact Disc Recording (17194)

Plush Toys
Small, adorable stuffed animals that become partners in learning with your child

Beethoven Bear (14654)
Mozart Mouse (14653)
Nannerl Mouse (18791)
Professor Haydn Hippo (18792)
J. S. Bunny (17216)
Clara Schumann-Cat (19767)
Puccini Pooch (17487)

Music for Little Mozarts
Christine H. Barden • Gayle Kowalchyk • E.L. Lancaster

Join Beethoven Bear, Mozart Mouse and their music friends as they learn about music. Follow their adventures from the Play Room and the Music Room to their Piano Lessons, their Music Class at school, the Talent Show and a Trip to the City.

Written to provide appropriate piano instruction for 4-, 5- and 6-year-olds, this series is a comprehensive approach to musical learning that develops singing and listening skills simultaneously with an appreciation for a variety of musical styles. The materials in the course combine to create an exciting and imaginative atmosphere both in the lesson and at home.

Music Lesson Books
Keyboard performance and introduction of music concepts
Book 1 (14577)   Book 3 (17180)
Book 2 (14581)   Book 4 (17186)

Music Workbooks
Coloring and ear training activities reinforcing music concepts
Book 1 (14580)   Book 3 (17181)
Book 2 (14584)   Book 4 (17187)

Music Discovery Books
Singing, listening, music appreciation, movement and rhythm activities
Book 1 (14579)   Book 3 (17182)
Book 2 (14583)   Book 4 (17188)

Music Recital Books
Performance repertoire
Book 1 (19724)   Book 2 (19725)

Coloring Books
Imaginative, music adventure pages to color
Book 1 (19669)   Book 3 (19671)
Book 2 (19670)   Book 4 (19672)

Halloween Fun!
A Halloween story with performance music and related music activity pages
Book 1 (20657)   Book 2 (20658)

Christmas Fun!
A Christmas story with performance music and related music activity pages
Book 1 (19720)   Book 2 (19721)

Lesson Assignment Book
Assignment pages, practice records, lesson evaluations and more
Lesson Assignment Book (17488)

Teacher's Handbooks
Lesson plans and teaching tips that are useful to parents and teachers
Books 1 & 2 (14585)   Books 3 & 4 (17192)

Alfred
Alfred Publishing Co., Inc.
16320 Roscoe Blvd., Suite 100
P.O. Box 10003
Van Nuys, CA 91410-0003
alfred.com

20657 $4.99

0 38081 19679 4

ISBN 0-7390-2706-9

T4-AGP-468